The Beautiful Ride

(A Jesusbride Collection)

The Beautiful Ride

Author: Olubukayo Oladunjoye

Copyright © Olubukayo Oladunjoye (2024)

The right of Olubukayo Oladunjoye to be identified as author of this work has been asserted by the author in accordance with section 77 and 78 of the Copyright, Designs and Patents Act 1988.

First Published in 2024

ISBN 978-1-83538-408-4 (Paperback)
978-1-83538-409-1 (Hardback)

Book Cover Design and Layout by:
White Magic Studios
www.whitemagicstudios.co.uk

Published by:
Maple Publishers
Fairbourne Drive, Atterbury,
Milton Keynes,
MK10 9RG, UK
www.maplepublishers.com

A CIP catalogue record for this title is available from the British Library.

All rights reserved. No part of this book may be reproduced or translated by any form or by any means, electronic or mechanical, including photocopying, recording or by any information storage and retrieval system without written permission from the author.

The views expressed in this work are solely those of the author and do not reflect the opinions of Publishers, and the Publisher hereby disclaims any responsibility for them.

Foreward

This booklet was created from excerpts from lengthy and inspired conversation between childhood friends which spanned over months after they reconnected online after a period of separation over 20 years.

These friendships re-surfaced shortly after the loss of a confidant in the person of a beloved and dear Grandma.

User Guide

Use this workbook to develop your own thoughts into a unique and meaningful plan or story by following the steps below:

- **Read meditatively through each picture story and collect your first thoughts on the authors' ideas and encounter.**
- **Then work through each picture story, noting down your own thoughts be it on a desired change, a dream vacation, an evangelistic outreach or a life goal.**
- **Note down reference scriptures, wise sayings and adages in support of your thoughts.**
- **Sum this all up and you soon realize that you are not far from creating your own story or desired life goal!**

I wish you a beautiful experience as you read and work through.

Beautiful Ride

Without the dream, there can be no destination!

Beautiful Ride

New waves mean new glory!

Live, love, and learn,

That is why Jesus came!

Beautiful Ride

I learned today that the driver and captain are not the same people.
You be the captain
and let Jesus be the driver.

Beautiful Ride

"The person behind the wheel of your life determines your destination, not the vehicle you're in."

Beautiful Ride

When you are committed to
Jesus Christ,
you will be experiencing
the Jehovah Overdo!

Beautiful Ride

Things can only get better.
When love is the expressway, you will be experiencing The Beautiful Ride!

Beautiful Ride

Childhood friends can do better when their best effort and focus are applied in love!

Beautiful Ride

When we make
people feel good,
then we introduce the
source of good
feelings.
We have turned them
into better people.
Our source is
the owner of all,
King Jesus!

Your Thoughts:

Reference: *(Scriptures/Adages/Quotes):*

'NOW CREATE YOUR OWN STORY'

Beautiful Ride

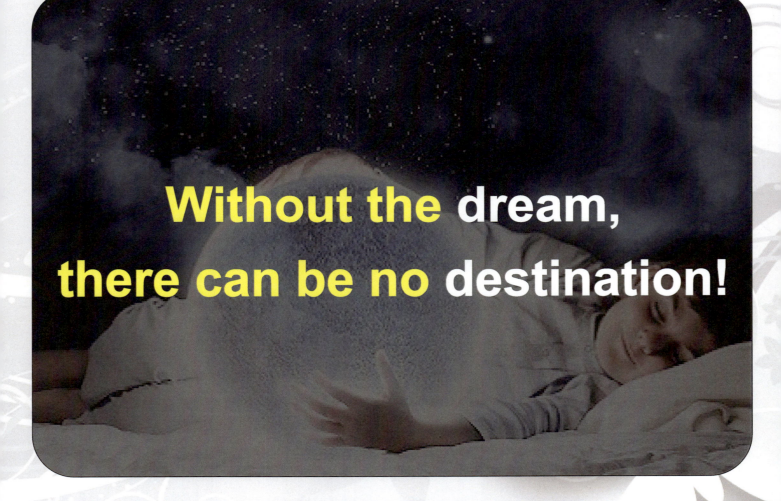

Without the dream, there can be no destination!

Your Thoughts:

Reference: *(Scriptures/Adages/Quotes):*

Beautiful Ride

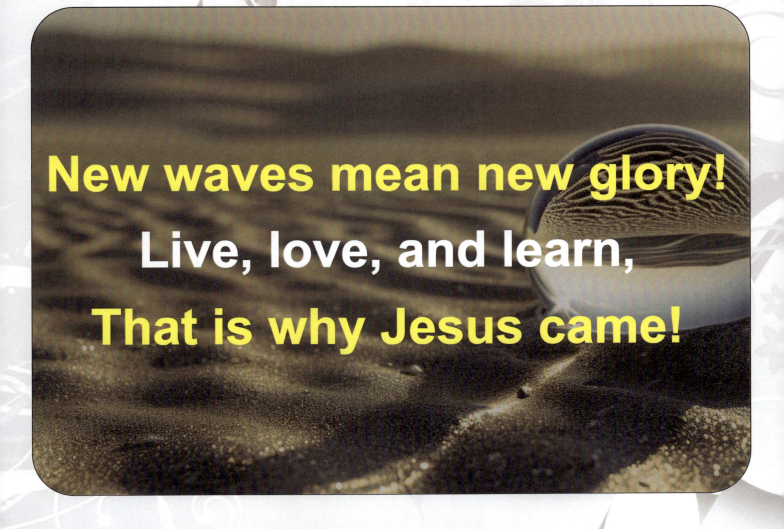

**New waves mean new glory!
Live, love, and learn,
That is why Jesus came!**

Your Thoughts:

_____
_____
_____
_____
_____
_____
_____
_____
_____
_____
_____
_____
_____

Reference: *(Scriptures/Adages/Quotes):*

_____
_____
_____
_____
_____

Beautiful Ride

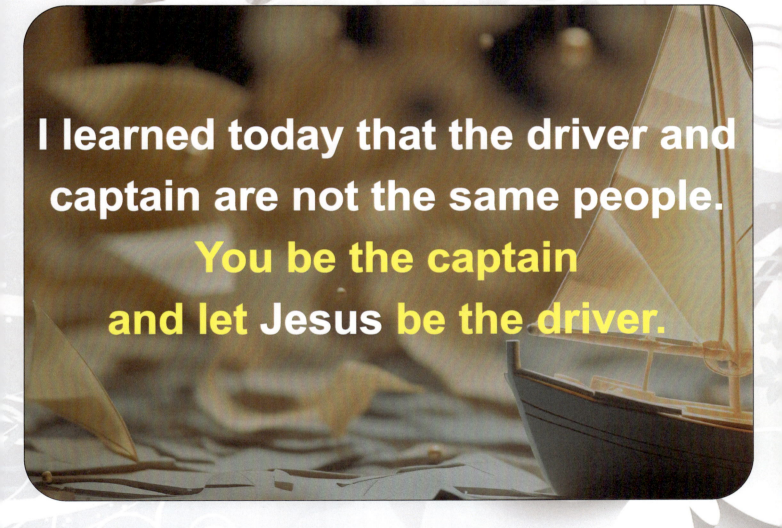

I learned today that the driver and captain are not the same people.

You be the captain and let Jesus be the driver.

Your Thoughts:

Reference: *(Scriptures/Adages/Quotes):*

Beautiful Ride

"The person behind the wheel of your life determines your destination, not the vehicle you're in."

Your Thoughts:

Reference: *(Scriptures/Adages/Quotes):*

Beautiful Ride

When you are committed to Jesus Christ, you will be experiencing the *Jehovah Overdo!*

Your Thoughts:

Reference: *(Scriptures/Adages/Quotes):*

Beautiful Ride

Things can only get better. When *love* is the expressway, you will be experiencing

The Beautiful Ride!

Your Thoughts:

Reference: *(Scriptures/Adages/Quotes):*

Beautiful Ride

Childhood friends can do better when their best effort and focus are applied in love!

Your Thoughts:

Reference: *(Scriptures/Adages/Quotes):*

Beautiful Ride

When we make people feel good,
then we introduce the source
of good feelings.
We have turned them into better people.
Our source is the owner of all,

King Jesus!

Your Thoughts:

___

Reference: *(Scriptures/Adages/Quotes):*

___

Acknowledgment

The authors and the graphic illustrator; Mrs. Olubukayo Oladunjoye (nee Oyetayo), Prince Adeyemi Olurin and Mr. Tolulope Folorunso dedicate this work to the love of God, the love of His Dear son Jesus Christ, to memories of our childhood days and the memories and honour of our loved ones.

Have you been able to successfully create your story with the aid of this guide? and do you want to share you thoughts with the authors? or provide feedback? please complete the response form via the link:

.https://forms.gle/fsKXp2YW446GzXHQA

or scan the QR code below:

www.ingramcontent.com/pod-product-compliance
Ingram Content Group UK Ltd.
Pitfield, Milton Keynes, MK11 3LW, UK
UKRC030805190225
455311UK00005B/15